Charles E. Forque & James

Harmonized Rhythms

For Concert Band

Progressive Melodic Rhythm Studies

NEIL A. KJOS MUSIC CO.

kjos

PUBLISHER

FOREWORD

It was pleasing for me to learn about **HARMONIZED RHYTHMS**. As a professional musician I realize the importance of rhythmic precision in the pursuit of quality musical performances. To play with excellent pitch and musical style is wonderful; however, without emphasis on the importance of rhythmic precision it will be difficult for an instrumentalist to perform successfully with others.

Playing with precision does not come naturally for many players. After students pass the beginning stages, they must be trained to think and feel the pulse of the beat! Understanding how different rhythmic patterns work together is a prerequisite to successful performances. The approach taken in **HARMONIZED RHYTHMS** is an excellent way to develop mental concentration, which is the key to playing with precision.

This book stresses the development of "**PULSE**" or **subdivision**. In all playing - jazz, classical, Latin, professional or amateur this "**pulse**" is a must for a really good performance. In all my years of playing I have found no exception to this rule. The fact that the exercises are melodic and scored with four part harmony is unique. This musical setting for rhythm studies is an enjoyable way to maintain student interest while they learn a most important aspect required for quality musical performance. Including the mallet and percussion players in all the studies is a very sound idea.

I congratulate the composers for their efforts in developing these much needed rhythmic study exercises for school bands. Directors and students alike will enjoy the new melodies and excellent harmonic scoring found in each exercise.

Best wishes to you and your students for continued success in the pursuit of quality band programs in our public and private schools.

Sincerely,

'Doc' Severinsen

p.s. I have known Charles Forque for over 28 years and have been witness to his great success as a music educator. Any advice he has to give should be accepted readily and enthusiastically.

CONTENTS

ISBN 0-8497-8542-1

To the Students,

Welcome to **HARMONIZED RHYTHMS**. The major objective in writing this book is to provide you with a method that progressively increases your **RHYTHMIC INDEPENDENCE**. An important aspect of "making music" is the challenge of **keeping the beat** while playing different rhythm patterns. This means playing your part so it "fits" with other parts being played at the same time. Playing with pulse is a MENTAL PROCESS. Understanding this process and the role that pulses of the beats play in the performance of music is critical. Learning to "mentally feel" the pulse is not difficult.

It is important for you to learn to do the counting! Remember, understanding and playing with pulse is the secret to "keeping the beat." If you learn the basic concepts that we emphasize in **HARMONIZED RHYTHMS** you will never have to ask your director "how does it go" or "sing it for me."

DUPLE AND TRIPLE - THE TWO BASIC PULSES
A BEAT IN MUSIC IS THE KIND OF NOTES THAT GETS ONE COUNT

In **HARMONIZED RHYTHMS** the **note** that receives a **beat** in duple meters is a **quarter note**. The pulse of each beat is **DUPLE** or two eighth notes to each quarter note. Look at the Rhythm Chart on page 5 and you will see the relationship between **two eighth notes** and a **quarter note**, the beat note. Duple pulse time signatures used in **HARMONIZED RHYTHMS** are 2/4, 3/4 and 4/4.

In triple meters the note that receives a **beat** is a **dotted quarter note**. The pulse of each beat is **TRIPLE** or three eighth notes to each dotted quarter note. Look at the Rhythm Chart on page 15 and you will see the relationship between three eighth notes and a dotted quarter note, the beat note. Triple pulse time signatures are 3/8, 6/8, 9/8 and 12/8.

The quarter note, dotted quarter note, and eighth notes are the only **beat notes** used in this book. However, you should know that there are instances when composers have used other kinds of notes as beat notes. Even then the beat pulses would be duple or triple.

Perhaps you have not heard the word pulse used in a musical setting. Your first question might be "what does it mean." When you played eighth notes for the first time your director taught you about subdivision. **PULSE** is a word that means the same thing as subdivision. Pulse suggests "being alive." **Music comes alive** through a **strong rhythmic pulse**. You must learn to mentally feel the pulse every time you play a note in music. The ticking of a clock and the beating of your heart assures you that they are working - so must your mental pulse be working for making music that is alive.

Best wishes for your continued musical growth.

Charles E. Forque and James Thornton

DUPLE RHYTHM CHART

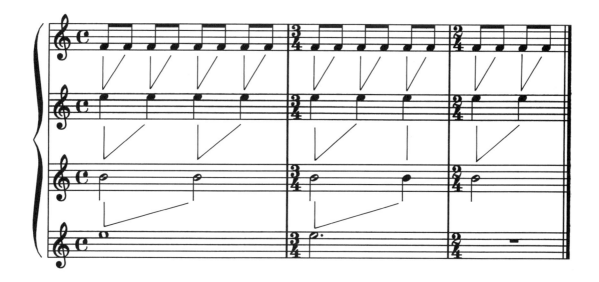

DUPLE BEATS AND PULSE

As you study the Duple Rhythm Chart above you will see that the quarter note is the BEAT NOTE and the eighth note is the PULSE NOTE. You can also see that the relationship from one staff to the other is always two to one. Precision, which means everyone getting to each beat together regardless of the kind of notes you have, is the key to successful playing. Be sure to use the counting system that your director has taught you when counting any exercise in this book.

It is important for you to **mentally feel** the pulse of the beat in every note that you play. A close study of the chart above clearly shows that a whole note is eight pulses long. By carrying this thought further it becomes obvious that a half note is four pulses long and a quarter note is two pulses long. Playing in your band will become more enjoyable as your band learns to **mentally feel** the pulse of the beat.

EXERCISE NO. 1

EXERCISE NO. 2

EXERCISE NO. 3

EXERCISE NO. 4

EXERCISE NO. 5

EXERCISE NO. 6

EXERCISE NO. 7

EXERCISE NO. 8

EXERCISE NO. 9

TRIPLE RHYTHM CHART

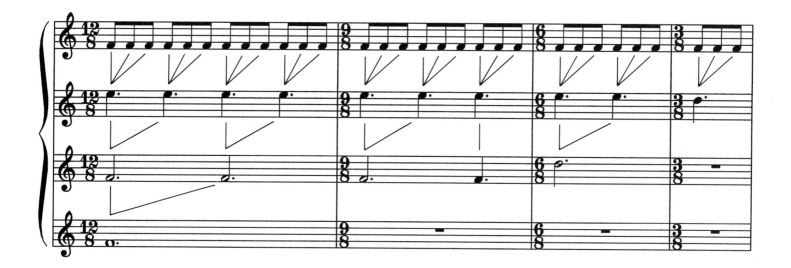

TRIPLE BEATS AND PULSES

As you study the Triple Rhythm Chart above you need to realize that except for the eighth notes, all the others are **dotted notes**. The dotted quarter note is the BEAT NOTE and three eighth notes are the PULSE NOTES. When you compare the relationship of one staff to another, realize that each beat is TRIPLE. This means that each beat has a pulse of three eighth notes (three being triple).

Study the staffs for a moment. You can clearly see the relationship from one staff to another is always three to one--triple.

- Three eighth notes = a dotted quarter note (the beat note).
- Six eighth notes or three quarter notes = a dotted half note.
- Twelve eighth notes or three half notes = a dotted whole note.

Unlike duple meters where there are two pulses to a beat, triple meters are built on three pulses to each beat. Using the counting system that your director has taught, verbally count beats with two pulses to each beat (eighth notes), and three pulses to each beat (eighth notes). This will teach you the difference between DUPLE and TRIPLE and how each one "feels."

EXERCISE NO. 10

EXERCISE NO. 11

EXERCISE NO. 12

EXERCISE NO. 13

EXERCISE NO. 14

EXERCISE NO. 15

EXERCISE NO. 16

EXERCISE NO. 17

EXERCISE NO. 18

EXERCISE NO. 19

EXERCISE NO. 20

EXERCISE NO. 21

EXERCISE NO. 22

EXERCISE NO. 23

EXERCISE NO. 24

EXERCISE NO. 25

EXERCISE NO. 26

EXERCISE NO. 27

34

EXERCISE NO. 28

W18TB

EXERCISE NO. 29

EXERCISE NO. 30

EXERCISE NO. 31

EXERCISE NO. 32

EXERCISE NO. 33

EXERCISE NO. 34

EXERCISE NO. 35

EXERCISE NO. 36

EXERCISE NO. 37

EXERCISE NO. 38

EXERCISE NO. 39

EXERCISE NO. 40

EXERCISE NO. 41

ODD METER RHYTHM CHART

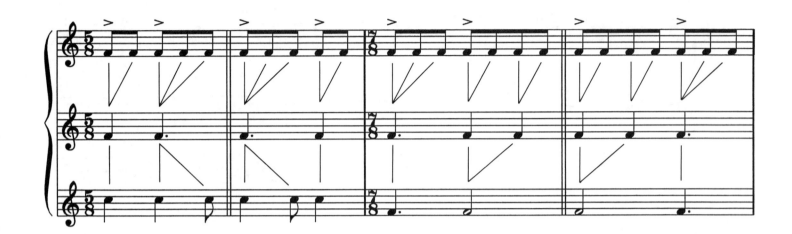

ODD METER BEATS

Odd meters are unique because they are a combination of both duple and triple. At a slow tempo the eighth note is the BEAT NOTE and a sixteenth note becomes the PULSE NOTE. If the tempo is faster one beat is a quarter note and the other beat is a dotted quarter note and the eighth note is the pulse note. A careful study of the rhythm chart above clearly outlines the structure of simple odd meter measures.

5/8 is written either 2 + 3 or 3 + 2. In **HARMONIZED RHYTHMS** we use only two of the three combinations for 7/8. Most common for 7/8 is 3 + 4 or 4 + 3. The combination not used in this book is 2 + 3 + 2.

Notice that accents have been placed over the groupings in both time signatures. They are there to assist you as you count the rhythms. Count each measure as follows:

	5/8	
One two **One** two three	or	**One** two three **One** Two
	7/8	
One two three **One** two three Four	or	**One** two three four **One** two three

Odd meters are fun to play and will challenge your ability to concentrate.

EXERCISE NO. 42

EXERCISE NO. 43

EXERCISE NO. 44

EXERCISE NO. 45

W18TB

THE COMPOSERS

CHARLES E. FORQUE

Charles Forque, a native Texan, retired in 1990 after a thirty-nine year career as a Director of Bands in Texas. The majority of his teaching career was spent in Plano, Texas at Plano Senior High School, and in Baytown, Texas at Robert E. Lee High School. The bands made a number of appearances at national and state clinics and conventions. The 1981 Plano band and the 1977 Robert E. Lee band presented the final concerts at the NORTHWEST BAND AND CHORAL CLINIC in Moorhead, Minnesota.

Charles received his Bachelors (1952) and his Masters (1971) degrees from Sam Houston State University. He has presented clinics throughout the United States and Canada and is still active as a clinician for high school bands in Texas. He has conducted summer camp bands at a number of universities including the Universities of Kansas, Wisconsin, Sam Houston State, Lamar, and Northwestern University in Louisiana. Numerous soloists have made appearances with his bands, including 'Doc' Severinsen, who performed 43 concerts with Charles' bands during their 28-year friendship. Charles is now the conductor of the Plano Community Band.

Joining with author Bruce Pearson, Charles and Gerald Anderson served as co-authors of the internationally successful beginning band method BEST IN CLASS and ENCORE FOR BAND. Charles is the author of CREATIVE CONCEPTS FOR MARCHING BANDS. He and his wife Ednajo have one daughter and two grandchildren.

JAMES THORNTON

Jim Thornton retired in 1991 after a forty-year career in music. He spent the first twenty-one years as a band director in Colorado, a professor of music and bassoonist in the faculty quintets at the University of New Mexico, and Illinois State University. Jim played bassoon professionally in the Dayton, Cincinnati, Albuquerque and Bloomington Orchestras. He has a Masters Degree from the Cincinnati Conservatory of Music. He is a member of the national honorary society Pi Kappa Lambda.

Jim is the author of books for woodwinds, an ear training method for band, and articles for THE INSTRUMENTALIST, MUSIC EDUCATORS JOURNAL, SOUTHWESTERN MUSICIAN, and the NACWPI JOURNAL. He has also written original compositions and arrangements for band including POEM by Griffes, Ravel's THE ENCHANTED GARDEN, and two wind pieces by Mozart. He is widely recognized as an expert in the field of tuning and intonation.

From 1972 until his retirement Jim was associated with the music industry as a school representative and music store manager in Dallas and Boston. He and his wife Mary live in Plano, Texas. They are the parents of five children, and proud grandparents of twelve grandchildren.